I Love Roc (+ cats)!

DATES IN THE STATES

A COUPLE TRAVELING THE UNITED
STATES ON A BUDGET

Mystery Date
Rochester, NY

By Dates in the States

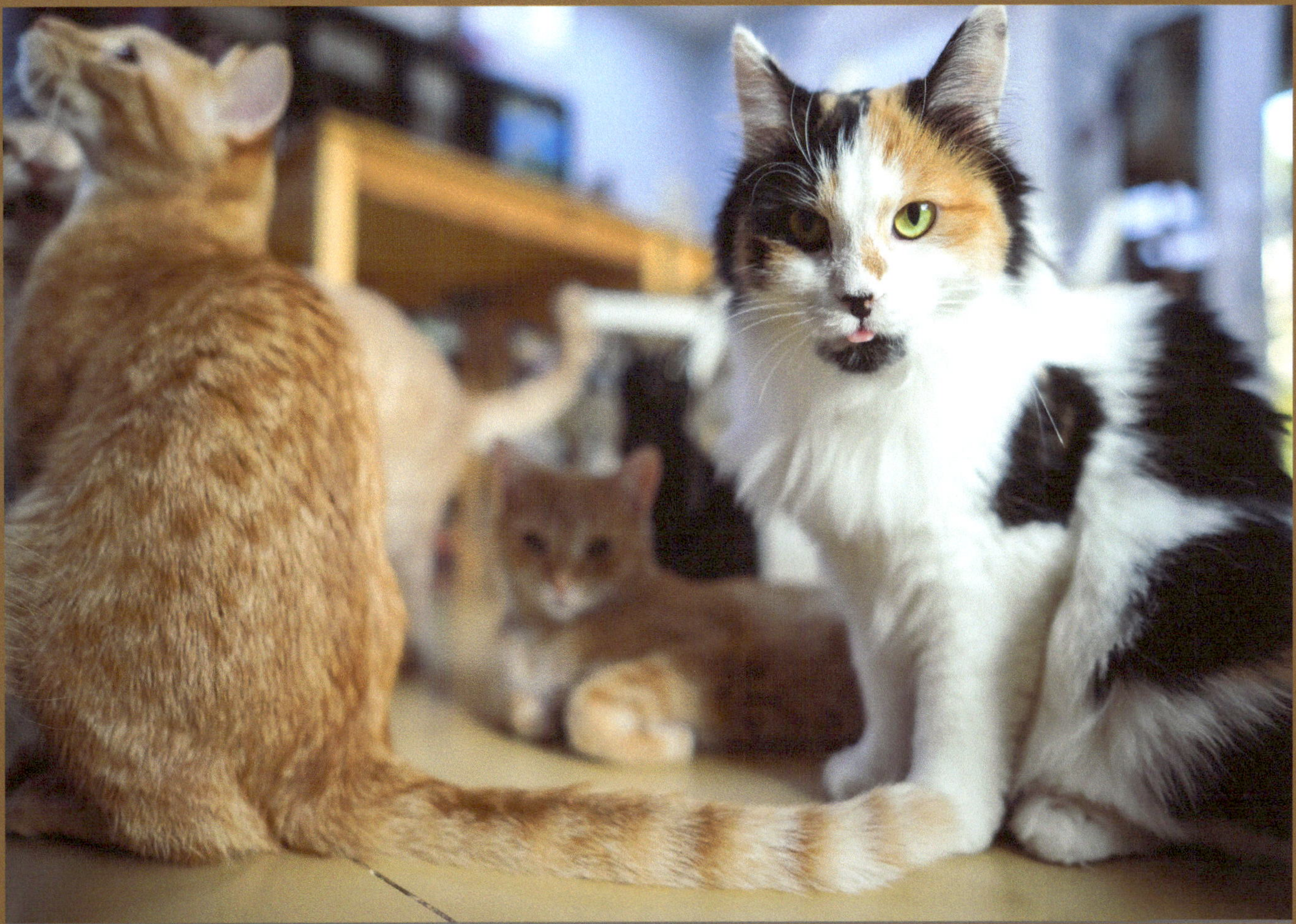

"Our passion is travel, and we want to share our adventures to inspire others to explore the world with their loved ones. Dare to live beyond the box."

Dates in the States

Introduction

Hey there! We're Crystal and Shane, the duo behind Dates in the States, where we share our love for discovering unique adventures, unforgettable moments, and hidden gems across the U.S. Whether you're searching for a fun date idea, a new place to explore, or just a little inspiration, we've got you covered!

Our Mystery Date Books are designed to help couples (and adventurous friends!) shake up their routine and experience the best local spots in a fun, intentional way. Inside, you'll find a curated collection of date ideas—each one meant to be completed over the course of a single day in a specific neighborhood. All of which are a surprise until you flip the page!

It's like a little challenge to break out of your comfort zone, support local, and make memories that stick. We hope this book helps you laugh more, explore more, and connect more—with each other and with your city. Let the mystery begin!

OUR RESIDENT CATS

Greta

Nova

Onyx

Chester

Here's What To Expect:

This Mystery Date blends creativity, coziness, and a touch of feline fun—all in one of Rochester's most vibrant neighborhoods. You'll kick things off at a local art center, soaking in inspiring exhibits before heading to a hidden gem of a bookstore. Next, unwind with some adoptable furry friends at a cozy cat café.

Take a quick stroll to one of the city's most iconic photo spots, then wrap up your adventure with a delicious meal at a lively downtown food hall.

Whether you're with your partner, a friend, or going solo, this date is all about local gems, feel-good moments, and making memories.

Whether you're out with your partner, your bestie, or flying solo, this mystery date offers the purr-fect blend of art, books, cats, and great food—all in one unforgettable local adventure.

START

RoCo Art Center

137 East Ave.
Rochester, NY 14604

Uncover a world of modern art and creativity with a mystery date at the Rochester Contemporary Art Center! Known for its bold exhibitions and unique cultural vibe, RoCo is the perfect place to enjoy an immersive date while exploring thought-provoking pieces together.

Plan to arrive during their limited hours: Wednesday through Sunday from 12-5 PM, and extend your experience with their First Friday receptions, when RoCo stays open until 9 PM. Stroll hand-in-hand through vibrant displays, share your interpretations, and pick your favorite artwork to discuss after.

2nd Stop

Greenwood Books

123 East Ave.
Rochester, NY 14604

Step into the cozy charm of Greenwood Books and explore the shelves together. Pick a section of the bookstore, and each of you find a book that catches your eye. Share the first paragraph or an interesting passage, and talk about why you chose it. Whether it's a rare find or a quirky gem that reminds you of each other, Greenwood Books is the perfect spot to bond over your love of books—or to discover something new together. Say hello to the owner, Franlee Frank, who brings her decades of experience to help guide customers not only to the books they're seeking but also to unexpected treasures they'll likely enjoy.

3rd Stop

Pawsitive Cat Cafe

120 East Ave. Ste 100, Rochester, NY 14604

Get ready for a purr-fect mystery date at Pawsitive Cat Café! Step into a cozy, feline-filled sanctuary where you and your date can sip coffee, snack on treats, and unwind alongside some friendly (and adoptable) cats. Whether you're a cat lover or just looking for a unique experience, this hidden gem offers a relaxing space to bond over cuddly kitties and conversations. Just remember to make an appointment online to reserve your time with the cats! Who knows—your date might not be the only one stealing your heart!

*For every mystery date book purchased at Pawsitive Cat Cafe, we'll donate $5 to support the cats and their cozy home.

4th Stop

I Love Roc Sign
291 East Main St,
Rochester, NY 14604

On your way to the final stop of your date, take a moment to walk by the iconic I Love ROC sign. It's the perfect spot to pause, snap a photo, and capture a bit of Rochester's charm before wrapping up your adventure together.

Last Stop

Mercantile on Main

240 East Main St,
Rochester, NY 14604

Wrap up your date at Mercantile on Main, a vibrant food hall with a variety of local dining options perfect for any craving. After your stop at the I Love ROC sign, head over to explore the food stalls and pick out dinner together.

From handcrafted pizzas to international bites, Mercantile on Main offers plenty of choices to satisfy any taste—making it a laid-back, fun way to finish your night in the heart of Rochester.

Alternative Dinner Stop

Stromboli's Restaurant

130 East Ave.

Rochester, NY 14604

If you're not in the mood for a food hall-style setting and would rather dig into a cheesy slice of pizza, Stromboli's is a must. This laid-back local favorite serves up delicious New York-style pies and hearty strombolis, with both indoor and outdoor seating that's perfect for a chill dinner. Their pizza is flavorful without being heavy—they offer gluten-free and dairy-free options, and on some nights, you might even catch some live music while you eat. A relaxed and satisfying way to wrap up your date!

Add Your Photos

Keepsakes

Thank you for joining us on this mystery date adventure! We hope you've enjoyed the delightful experiences and memorable moments we've crafted just for you in Rochester, NY.

But the adventure doesn't stop here! Keep exploring exciting mystery dates in other cities and uncover new romantic experiences across the U.S. by visiting our website, DatesInTheStates.com. There, you can purchase both physical copies and digital downloads of our mystery date books. Plus, don't miss out on our Mystery Date Book Club, where you can receive a brand-new mystery date book every month!

Tag us in your date photos on social media! @datesinthestates

About the Creators

Crystal, the writer and creator, is a storyteller at heart. When she's not uncovering hidden gems for the next date night idea, she runs her own digital marketing company, helping small businesses improve their content marketing, increase visibility in their communities, and streamline their online presence.
Visit: crystalstatskey.com

Shane, her husband and partner in adventure, is a dedicated personal trainer and the owner of Beekstar Fitness in Irondequoit, NY. He specializes in working with clients who have limited mobility, helping them build muscle and focus on pain areas so they can regain strength and confidence in their daily lives.
Visit: beekstarfitness.com

Crystal and Shane have explored every U.S. state except Alaska (coming soon!) and are now visiting countries in alphabetical order. Whether road-tripping or curating Mystery Date experiences, they're always chasing their next adventure.

Local Love

A few local gems in Rochester
worth exploring on your next date.

THE LITTLE THEATRE
MOVIE THEATER FEATURING INDIE FILMS
240 EAST AVE, ROCHESTER, NY 14604

UGLY DUCK COFFEE
CHILL COFFEE SHOP
89 CHARLOTTE ST, ROCHESTER, NY 14607

HE STRONG NATIONAL MUSEUM OF PLAY
YOU'RE NEVER TOO OLD FOR THIS PLACE!
1 MANHATTAN SQUARE DR, ROCHESTER, NY 14607

Want to see your business here?
See the next page for details on
how to join!

Want to be featured?

MYSTERY DATE BOOK PACKAGES

—

Are you a small business looking to reach new customers? Feature your business in our next Mystery Date Book! Choose from our partnership packages below to connect with couples seeking unique experiences and exclusive deals.

Package One
LOCAL LOVE LISTING

—

A quick shoutout to show you're part of the neighborhood vibe.

Listed in the "Local Love" section of your designated neighborhood date book

Includes business name, address, and social link

Optional: Offer a small promo (e.g., 10% off for book holders)

1 social media shout-out when the book launches

$45

Package Two
FEATURE STOP

—

You're not just a business— you're part of the experience.

Marked as a "Must-Stop" on a Mystery Date

Full-page feature in the book with your story, offerings and photo

Includes 1 social media feature — a dedicated post and story highlighting your business

Note: To ensure each feature is genuine and experience-based, we require a hosted visit prior to inclusion.

$95

Package Three
PARTNER & SELLER

—

Be the spot and the source.

Everything in Tier 2

PLUS: Option to sell the Mystery Date Books at your location

Includes a bulk purchase of 10 books (yours to price + sell)

Keep 100% of the profits from in-store sales

Bonus: Tag as an official pickup location in our promotions

$150

Prices are subject to change

Feel free to reach us at any time by sending us an email to say hi and to learn more! We look forward to hearing from you.

| www.datesinthestates.com | datesinthestatesblog@gmail.com |

Sponsors & Affiliates

Our sponsors and affiliates help make our adventures possible! Explore the amazing brands and businesses that support our community.

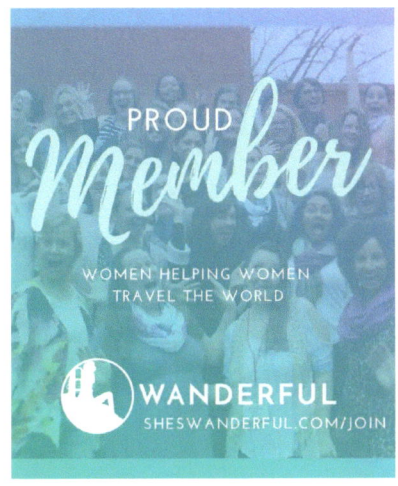

Wanderful

Wanderful is a global community for women who love to travel. Connect, explore, and join a local hub near you!

Join our Book Club!

Join our Mystery Date Book Club and be part of a travel-inspired community, discovering unique local adventures together!

HomeExchange

HomeExchange lets you swap homes with travelers worldwide for authentic, affordable stays. Join today and travel differently!

Shop our books at a store near you!

Little Button Craft
658 South Ave.
Rochester, NY 14620

The Pawsitive Cat Cafe
120 East Ave. Ste 100
Rochester, NY 14604

Yesterday's Muse Books
32 West Main St.
Webster, NY 14580

Writers & Books
740 University Ave,
Rochester, NY 14607

Littleberger Florist
63 North Avenue,
Webster, NY 14580

Flight Wine Bar
262 Exchange Blvd,
Rochester, NY 14608

Scents by Design
728 University Ave,
Rochester, NY 14607

Union Tavern
4565 Culver Rd,
Irondequoit, NY 14622

DATES IN THE STATES

A COUPLE TRAVELING THE UNITED STATES ON A BUDGET

Contact Us

datesinthestates.com

datesinthestatesblog@gmail.com

Based in Rochester, NY

CONNECT WITH US ON SOCIAL!

@DATESINTHESTATES